Noybel's Kitchen Cuban Flair Plant Based Cuisine

Copyright © 2016 by Noybel Gorgoy Reyes.

Photographs by:

Chris Tollette Photography

Editing by:

Shelley Tollette

All Rights Reserved. No part of this publication may be reproduced, stored, distributed, or transmitted in any form or by any means, including photocopying, recording, or other electronic or mechanical methods, photocopying, recording, without the prior written permission of the publisher, except in the case of brief quotations embodied in critical reviews and certain other noncommercial uses permitted by copyright law.

IBSN:978-0-9984028-2-6 (Create Space version)

Published By Noybel's Kitchen

www.noybelskitchen.com

Chris Tollette's photography Gallery:

https://christollettephotography.smugmug.com

The content in this book has not been evaluated by the FDA and is not intended to diagnose, treat, heal or prevent any disease.

TABLE OF CONTENT

Preface: What is the book about?	5
Introduction : My personal journey with Plant Based Foods	6
Turmeric Mango Crepe with Coconut Butter	9
The Matcha, Cacao, Strawberry Crepe	13
Cuban Queen Guava Smoothie	16
Carrot Pasta in a Coconut Sauce	18
Fennel Me Watermelon Radish Salad	22
Creamy Fennel Me Amaranth	25
Fermented Seed Cheese	28
Lobster Mushroom Lentil Tacos with Chipotle Sauce	31
Garbanzo con Nopales	35
Inspiration of India	38
Pumpkin Creamy Malanga	42
Cream of Pumpkin and Mushrooms	45
Wake Salad and Fresh Persimmons	49
Kale Salad	52
Roasted Chlorella Cauliflower	55
Chocolate Covered Buñuelo Cookies	57
Omega 3 No Ice Cream- Ice Cream	62
Cacao Sweet Potato Brownies	64
Thank you Notes	68

WHAT IS THE BOOK ABOUT?

"Noybel's Kitchen, Cuban Flair Plant Based Cuisine," is a small introduction to gluten free, plant based foods from my ever expanding perspective.

My biggest goal with this book is to open the minds of as many individuals as possible, about the endless potential of plant based foods.

This book is a beautiful journey of my Cuban influences being transmuted into healthier plant based alternatives. Additionally, the book is a way of sharing new ideas that I have discovered through my evolution in cooking.

Within the pages, you will unwrap different interpretations of how to use various condiments. Hopefully, you will find the inspiration to transform each recipe into your own variation.

My sincere wish is through my plant based recipes; you will be motivated to add more fresh organic fruits, vegetables, and whole foods to your diet. Share the benefits of experiencing a healthier and more fulfilling life with your whole circle of friends and family members!

Stay healthy, stay inspired and always have fun in the process. Enjoy!

MY PERSONAL JOURNEY WITH PLANT BASED FOODS

I was born and raised in the Caribbean Island of Cuba. My birthplace is known for its colorful music, food, people, and culture. In my home, our kitchen was a place related to celebration, experimentation, family gatherings and the love between my parents.

Seasonal organic whole foods was a priority in my father's eyes. He loved nourishing the body through wholesome and delicious foods. My father was one of the best chefs and biggest inspirations in my life!

I was always involved in the kitchen assisting my mother in meal preparations, also. My mom was another grand influence in my life. Together, with my father, she created new dishes with only a few available ingredients. I marveled at their culinary ingenuity!

As the so-called special period hit Cuba in the 1990's, the situation for us became very difficult. Although we had money in our home, meat became a luxury commodity. Legumes became our main protein source. Sometimes a nice bowl of black bean soup was all we had to consume. I soon came to the understanding that I did not require animal proteins to feel like I had a satisfying and enjoyable meal.

After graduating from the National School of Arts in Havana, I began to fully discover the world of food and the art of experimenting with the various ingredients available. Traveling the world as a professional musician indeed provided me with different perceptions of numerous cultures and multiple ways of using one food ingredient.

When I arrived in America, I was overwhelmed by the diverse choices of foods. I found my health suffering as I sampled from various foods and their wide range of qualities. I decided to take my health back into my own hands and help others to understand the differences in their food choices.

I discovered a wealth of information as I became more curious about new ways to express my creative juices, in my kitchen. I felt even more inspired to help myself, loved ones and my future children. I enrolled and completed my Professional Plant Based Certification from Rouxbe Online Cooking School in 2015. A phenomenal course lead by world-renowned plant-based chef educator Chad Sarno.

Today, I am passionate about life, arts, health, the best foods available and health-giving nutrition.

My desire is to inspire others to fall in love with the Plant Kingdom and embark upon their own creative culinary adventure!

TURMERIC MANGO CREPE WITH COCONUT BUTTER

Ingredients:

Ingredients for Crepe Batter

1 cup of rice flour

1 cup of tapioca flour

1 tbsp of ground flax seeds

pinch of salt

2 drops of liquid stevia or maple syrup to taste

1 tbsp of alcohol-free vanilla extract or powder

1 tsp of turmeric powder

2 1/2 cups coconut milk

1 tbsp of coconut oil

Crepe Filling

1/2 cup of melted coconut butter

1 to 2 cups of diced fresh mangoes

small diced fresh persimmon for garnish

Mango Sauce

juice of 1/2 lemon

1 cup of diced fresh mangoes

1 splash of coconut milk if needed or enough to allow the blender to run smoothly and achieve a creamy consistency.

pinch of salt

add sweetener (if needed)

Instructions:

To begin the recipe, gather all the ingredients and organize your work area. Measure and pre-prep your recipe ingredients.

Gather and place crepe ingredients into a high powered blender. Blend ingredients until smooth.

Preheat a non-stick pan over medium high heat. When the pan is sufficiently warm, add 1 tsp of coconut oil and coat the entire pan.

Add approximately 1/3 cup of crepe batter and distribute the batter in a nice thin circular shape. You may add more batter, depending on the size of the crepes you desire.

Allow the crepe to cook for a few minutes. Once the underside of the crepe has cooked, flip the crepe and let the other side to finish cooking.

When crepe is completely cooked, place the crepe on a plate and prepare to serve.

Mango Sauce

To prepare the mango sauce, add sauce ingredients into a high powered blender. Blend mango sauce until smooth.

To assemble the crepe, place the crepe on a cutting board. Add 1 tbsp of melted coconut butter and 1 or 2 tbsp of the mango cream. Spread generously over the crepe.

Add freshly diced mangoes. Layer your filling ingredients in amounts suitable to your taste buds! Fold crepe in any fashion you like, have fun !!!

To serve, place the crepe on a plate, drizzle with more mango sauce and garnish with fresh persimmons.

Serves 4 crepes.

THE MATCHA CACAO, STRAWBERRY CREPE

Ingredients:

Ingredients for the Crepe Batter

1 cup of ground buckwheat
1 tbsp of ground flax seeds
pinch of salt
2 drops of liquid stevia
1 tbsp of alcohol-free vanilla extract or powder
1 tsp of matcha powder
1 tbsp of coconut oil or ghee butter
2 1/2 cups coconut milk

Crepe Filling

2 cups of freshly sliced strawberries
maple syrup for garnish

Cacao Cream Ingredients

2 cups of raw hazelnuts
4 tbsp of raw cacao powder
1 tsp of lemon juice
1/2 cup of coconut milk (optional)
1/3 cup of coconut oil
stevia or maple syrup to taste

Instructions:

   To begin the recipe, gather all the ingredients and organize your work area. Measure and pre-prep your recipe ingredients.

Gather and place crepe ingredients into a high powered blender. Blend ingredients until smooth.

On medium high heat, preheat a non-stick pan. Once the pan has sufficiently warmed, add 1 tsp of coconut oil or ghee butter. Make sure to coat all areas of the pan. Add approximately 1/3 cup of batter and distribute the batter in a nice thin circular shape. You may add more batter, depending on the size of the crepes you desire.

Allow the crepe to cook for a few minutes. When the underside of the crepe has cooked, flip the crepe and enable the other side to finish cooking.

When crepe is completely cooked, place the crepe on a plate and prepare to serve.

To prepare the cacao cream, start by toasting the hazelnuts in a pan on medium high heat. Stir constantly until the nuts have lightly browned.

Note- This step is optional as you may use your hazelnuts completely raw.

Once the hazelnuts are ready, remove the skins. Add the toasted nuts, with the remainder of your cacao paste ingredients into a high speed blender. Blend until smooth.

Note- Depending on the power of your blender, you may need to add more maple syrup or coconut milk .

To assemble the crepe, place the crepe on a cutting board. Add as much cacao cream as desired, and fill in the crepe with fresh organic strawberries. Layer your filling ingredients in amounts suitable to your taste buds!

Drizzle crepe with maple syrup and add a dash of cacao powder as a finishing touch to your Matcha Crepe!

Serves 4 crepes.

CUBAN QUEEN

GUAVA SMOOTHIE

Ingredients:

1 cup of fresh medium diced guayabas (red or white guavas)
2 cups of coconut milk or any other nut milk of your choice
a few drops of stevia or maple syrup or if needed
pinch of Himalayan salt
1 cup of ice (optional)
1 tsp of spirulina or chlorella for extra chlorophyll

Instructions:

To begin the recipe, gather all the ingredients and organize your work area. Measure and pre-prep your recipe ingredients.

Add all your ingredients into a high speed blender and blend until completely smooth. Keep in mind that Guayaba is a very creamy tropical fruit.
 Serve in a clear glass and enjoy!
 *Note - In Cuba we call Guayaba, the queen of all fruits for its taste and nutritional properties! The sweetness of this delicious fruit varies according to the country the fruit is produced.

Serves around 2.

CARROT PASTA IN A COCONUT SAUCE

Ingredients:

15 fresh carrots for noodles
3 mashed garlic cloves
Sea salt or Himalayan salt to taste
freshly ground black pepper to taste
freshly ground pink peppercorns to taste
1 tbsp of dried white wine or coconut aminos
1/2 cup of coconut cream
3 tbsp of vegetable broth, if needed
1 tbsp of capers
1 small diced ripe tomato
1 cup of fine chopped fresh dandelion greens
1/2 cup of fine chopped cilantro
fresh basil for garnish
Fresh chives and ground turnips for garnish

Instructions:

To begin the recipe, gather all the ingredients and organize your work area. Measure and pre-prep your recipe ingredients.

*Note- To make the carrot noodles use a spiralizer or any equipment which easily prepares the carrot noodles for you.

Heat a large pan over medium high heat. When the pan is hot, add the coconut oil or ghee butter, pressed garlic, salt, and pepper. Stir ingredients, allowing them to cook for 1 to 2 minutes.

Add the dried wine or coconut aminos until fully absorbed.

Next, add the capers, diced tomatoes and half of the coconut cream. Thoroughly mix all ingredients, keeping in mind that you want to achieve a creamy consistency. Feel free to add more liquid if needed.

Lower the heat, add the carrot noodles to the pan and mix well. Add the dandelion greens, fresh cilantro, and additional salt and pepper to taste. Allow it to cook for another minute.

To finish the dish, you may garnish with fresh basil, ground turnips, and pink peppercorns. You may also add any nuts or seeds for extra protein.

Serves around 2 plates.

FENNEL ME WATERMELON RADISH SALAD

Ingredients:

2 thin sliced fennel bulbs
1 thin sliced watermelon radish
red chili pepper flakes for garnish
lime wedges for garnish
fennel leaves for garnish
White Sauce
juice of 1 lime
1 cup of cashews
1 cup of water
1 garlic clove
1/3 cup small diced red onions
1 tbsp of apple cider vinegar
Sea salt or Himalayan salt to taste
freshly ground black pepper to taste

Instructions:

To begin the recipe, gather all the ingredients and organize your work area. Measure and pre-prep your recipe ingredients.

Next, add all the ingredients for the white sauce into a high speed blender and blend until smooth.

Add the thinly sliced fennel bulbs and watermelon radish to a mixing bowl, add 2 or 3 tbsp of the white sauce or as much as you desire and mix well.

Plate the salad and garnish the dish with small diced fennel Leaves, a wedge of lemon for a splash of freshness and red chili pepper flakes for extra heat.

Serve the salad with your favorite side dish, grain or protein.

Serves 2 plates.

CREAMY FENNEL ME AMARANTH

Ingredients:

2 thin sliced fennel bulbs

1 thin sliced watermelon radish

White Sauce

1 cup of cashews or macadamia nuts

1 cup of water

1 garlic clove

1/3 cup of diced red onions

1 tbsp of apple cider vinegar

salt to taste

freshly ground black pepper to taste

Amaranth

1 cup of amaranth

3 cups of vegetable stock

salt to taste

freshly ground pepper to taste

1 tsp of coconut oil

Instructions:

To begin the recipe, gather all the ingredients and organize your work area. Measure and pre- prep your recipe ingredients.

Place a small or medium size pot with the amaranth, flavorful liquid stock, coconut oil, salt and ground pepper on medium low heat. Bring to a boil. Allow the mixture to cook for approximately 15 to 25 minutes. Make sure to stir often. Keep in mind, depending on the humidity content of your area; you may need to add more liquid as the amaranth cooks.

Once the amaranth sprouts and some of the liquid has been absorbed, turn off the stove, cover the pot with a lid and allow it to rest.

Next, add all the ingredients for the white sauce into a high speed blender and blend until smooth.

Dice the fennel bulb into the desired size and add to a pan on medium heat. Add in as much sauce and amaranth as you wish to the pan of fennel. Mix well and allow ingredients to warm up, thoroughly.

Serve with thinly sliced watermelon radish and add your favorite sprouts for extra protein.

Serves 2 plates.

FERMENTED SEED CHEESE

Ingredients:

1 cup of your favorite seeds

water for soaking seeds

1 package of your favorite seed cheese starter

1 cup of additional water

Instructions:

   To begin the recipe, gather all the ingredients and organize your work area. Measure and pre-prep your recipe ingredients.

   Place seeds in a container, add enough water to cover seeds and soak overnight.

   The following day, drain your seeds. Add the seeds and 1/4 cup of water into a high speed blender. Blend the mixture until completely smooth, add the cheese starter and blend ones again. Add more of the remaining cup of water, if needed.

  *Note - The thicker the consistency of the mixture, the better. Add water in small increments.

Pour the batter into a cheesecloth and place it in a small colander. Twist the top of the cheesecloth to tightly enclose the mixture. Place the colander on top of a small bowl to catch any excess liquid.

Cover with a clean kitchen towel.

Leave the mixture overnight in a dark area with a temperature of 70 to 75 degrees. The following morning, remove the cheese from the cloth and place it into a small bowl.

Add fresh herbs, spices, sea salt and pepper flakes. Serve with your favorite raw crackers.

Serves 3 to 4 people.

LOBSTER MUSHROOM LENTIL TACOS WITH CHIPOTLE SAUCE

Ingredients:

1 cup of dehydrated or fresh wild lobster mushrooms

1 1/2 cup of water

1/2 cup small diced red onions

3 garlic cloves

One tsp of coconut oil

1/8 tsp of dried oregano

1/8 tsp of dried marjoram

salt to taste

freshly ground black pepper to taste

1 tbsp of dried wine or coconut aminos

1 cup of cooked french lentils

1 cup of your favorite sprouts

1 avocado

Non-GMO sprouted corn tortillas

Chipotle sauce

1 cup of pre-soaked cashews

the juice of 1 lime

1 garlic clove

1/2 cup of water

1/8 to 1/4 tsp of chipotle powder

Sea salt and fresh ground black pepper to taste

Instructions:

To begin the recipe, gather all the ingredients and organize your work area. Measure and pre-prep your recipe ingredients.

In a small container, add 1 1/2 cup of room temperature water and one cup of dehydrated lobster mushrooms. Allow them to soak and rehydrate for approximately 15 to 20 minutes.

Note- If your lobster mushrooms are fresh, omit this step.

Place a medium size non-stick pan on medium high heat. Add the coconut oil to the pan and allow it to melt.

To the oil, add the onions, salt, and freshly ground peppers. Cook until the onions start to become translucent, making sure to constantly stir the mixture. While onions continue to cook, mash the garlic cloves in a mortar and pestle. Add the lobster mushrooms to the pan, followed by dried herbs, spices, and mashed garlic. Add more coconut oil, if needed.

Allow this mixture to cook for 2 to 3 minutes, making sure to stir everything in the pan, frequently. Add the dried wine or coconut aminos and allow to become fully absorbed.

Continue stirring to ensure the entire mixture is coated thoroughly.

Add 1 half cup or the full cup, if desired, of the soaking water from your lobster mushrooms. Cover the pan and let the mushrooms cook until they completely absorb the added liquid.

Thin slice the avocado and pour the lentils into a separate container. Wash the sprouts and place in an additional small bowl.

Next, prepare the chipotle sauce. Place the ingredients for the chipotle sauce inside a high speed blender. Blend to a smooth consistency.

You are now ready to assemble the tacos.

Warm the Non-GMO tortillas, as desired. To each tortilla, add 1 or 2 tbsp of french lentils, add 3 or 4 slices of avocados, 1 tbsp of lobster mushrooms and toss on your favorite sprouts. To finish up, drizzle chipotle sauce all over, sprinkle with lime juice and freshly ground black pepper and enjoy!

Serves 6 to 8 small tacos.

GARBANZOS CON NOPALES

CACTUS LEAF GARBANZOS

Ingredients:

1 cup small diced red onions

2 mashed garlic cloves

1 small diced nopal cactus leaf

1/3 cup of poblano pepper

1 tsp of dried wine or coconut aminos

2 1/2 cup of precooked garbanzo beans

1 bay leaf

a pinch of dried oregano

1/2 tsp of cumin powder

1/2 tsp of turmeric powder

1/2 cup of small diced fresh tomatoes

2 small diced sun dried tomatoes

1 cup of coconut cream

1/2 cup of chopped fresh cilantro

1 tsp of coconut oil or ghee butter

3 cups of vegetable broth

Sea salt or Himalayan salt to taste

freshly ground black pepper to taste

Instructions:

To begin the recipe, gather all the ingredients and organize your work area. Measure and pre-prep your recipe ingredients.

In a medium size pot, pour 2 cups of the vegetable stock and bring it to a boil on medium high heat. Carefully remove the stems of the nopal cactus leaf and rinse well. Small dice the cactus leaf and add the pieces to the pot, allowing the cactus leaf to cook for approximately 5 minutes.

Once ready, remove the small diced cactus from the boiling pot, rinse with cold water and set aside.

Heat a large pan over medium low heat. Add the coconut oil or ghee butter, onions, poblano pepper, salt and ground black pepper. Allow the onions to cook for a minute or two until soft and translucent. Add the garlic and allow mixture to cook for a few more seconds.

Continue, by adding the nopal leaf, sun-dried tomatoes, spices, and dried herbs. Thoroughly combine the ingredients in the pan and allow to cook for another 2 to 3 minutes. Stir constantly to avoid burning any ingredient. Next, add the dried wine or coconut aminos and enable it to become fully incorporated. As you continue stirring the ingredients add the fresh tomatoes.

Add the garbanzo beans, salt and pepper to taste and coconut milk. Mix well and let garbanzos simmer for an additional 5 minutes on low heat.

When the mixture is ready to serve, add the fresh cilantro. Sprinkle with additional salt and pepper, if needed.

Serve with your favorite grain or salad. A wedge of lime and fresh avocado. Serves 3 to 4 plates.

INSPIRATION OF INDIA

Ingredients:

2 cups of roughly chopped kale

2 cups of spinach

1 cup of small diced shallots

1 cup of small diced potatoes

1 garlic clove

1 roasted red pepper

1 cup of your favorite beans

1 cup of rough chopped fresh cilantro

1 tsp of turmeric powder

1 tsp of cumin powder

1/2 tsp of fenugreek powder

1/4 tsp of cardamom powder

1/2 tsp of cinnamon powder

1 tsp of paprika

salt and freshly ground black pepper to taste

1 tsp of ghee butter or coconut oil

coconut milk

2 tsp of olive oil

cayenne pepper or any other hot peppers for extra heat (optional)

Instructions:

To begin the recipe, gather all the ingredients and organize your work area. Measure and pre-prep your recipe ingredients.

Small dice the potatoes and de-stem the kale leaves. Bring a medium size pot with 2 cups of water to a boil. Arrange diced potatoes on the first tray of a bamboo steamer and fill the second tray with the kale and spinach. Stack trays on top of the pot with boiling water and allowed the potatoes to steam until soft.

Steam the kale and spinach around 2 to 3 minutes or until they soften up, slightly. Make sure to keep an eye on the greens to avoid over cooking and to keep the vibrant green color within the vegetables.

Note- Always add more water, if needed, to avoid burning the pot.

Dice the shallots, cilantro and roasted red pepper.

Add the steamed greens to a food processor or a high powered blender, followed by the cilantro, garlic, roasted red pepper, olive oil and the salt and pepper to taste. Add a dash of coconut milk to allow ingredients to run through the blender, easily. Blend until smooth. Add more liquid, if needed, depending on your equipment. The sauce should be as thick or chunky as you desire, but definitely, not too runny.

Preheat the pan on a medium low heat and add coconut oil or ghee butter for sautéing.

Place the diced shallots in the pan and allowed them to cook for 2 to 3 minutes or until translucent. Make sure to constantly stir and move the shallots in this process.

Next, add in all the powdered spices and let them toast for 1 minute. If you desire extra heat in the dish, add the hot pepper of your choice to the mixture. Immediately afterward, pour the mix of blended greens and freshly ground black pepper into the pan. Stir until ingredients are well combined.

Add the remaining coconut milk, or the amount needed to reach your desired consistency. Follow with the steamed potatoes, precooked beans and salt and pepper, to taste. Cook for another 5 minutes.

Serve with any seed like grain, fermented vegetables or favorite side dish of yours!

Serves around 4 plates.

PUMPKIN CREAMY MALANGA

Ingredients

2 cups of medium diced malanga

2 1/2 cups of vegetable stock

2 garlic cloves

Sea salt or Himalayan salt to taste

freshly ground black pepper to taste

1/3 cup of coconut milk

1 cup of diced pumpkin

2 tbsp of coconut oil, olive oil or ghee butter

1 tsp of coconut aminos

Instructions:

To begin the recipe, gather all the ingredients and organize your work area. Measure and pre-prep your recipe ingredients.

Pour 2 to 3 cups of water into a medium size pot and bring to a boil over medium high heat. Arrange the diced pumpkin in a bamboo steamer. Place the steamer on top of the boiling pot of water and allow the pumpkin to steam for 5 to 10 minutes. You should be able to grab the diced pumpkin with a fork and it falls off, but do not over cook.

In a medium size pot, add the vegetable stock. Add in 1 clove of garlic, coconut milk, salt, and pepper. On medium low heat, allow this liquid to warm up.

When the liquid begins to boil, add the medium diced malangas. Make sure to add more vegetable stock to cover the malangas, if necessary.

Once the malangas are very soft, turn off the stove and carefully add the malangas and pumpkin to a high speed blender. Add in the remaining ingredients and as much liquid as needed to reach your desired consistency. Blend until smooth.

Serve your Pumpkin Creamy Malanga with a salad of your choice. To garnish, you may add a drizzle of a healthy infused herbal oil if available.

Note- Malanga is a very slippery root. Take precautions to make cutting safe.

Have fun and enjoy this delicious root that is part of our traditional Cuban cuisine.

Serves around 4 bowls.

CREAM OF PUMPKIN AND MUSHROOMS

Ingredients:

2 cups of mixed mushrooms (bunapi, champignons, white stuffers, whole crimini, and wild lobster mushrooms)

2 cups of medium diced pumpkin

1 cup chopped red onions

1 clove of mashed garlic

1/8 tsp of coriander

1/8 tsp of fenugreek

1/2 tsp of chipotle powder

1/2 tsp of turmeric powder

2 tbsp of coconut aminos

1 pinch of freshly ground nutmeg

1 cup of coconut milk

3 cups of water or homemade vegetable broth

rehydrating water from the wild lobster mushrooms

1 tsp of coconut oil or ghee butter

Sea salt to and fresh ground black pepper taste

Instructions:

To begin the recipe, gather all the ingredients and organize your work area. Measure and pre-prep your recipe ingredients.

If using dehydrated mushrooms, add approximately 1 cup of mushrooms to 1 cup of water in a small container. Allow them to rehydrate for around 20 minutes or so. Ensure that you save the rehydrating water. You may add it to the cream for a richer flavor profile!

Place a large pot on medium high heat and add the coconut oil. Once the oil has melted, add the onions and allow them to cook for a minute, until soft. Begin adding in the ingredients, rehydrated mushrooms, spices, and followed by the medium diced pumpkin and the garlic.

Let the mixture cook for another 2 minutes. Stir constantly to allow the mushrooms to cook fully and all the oils and aromas to be released.

Next, add the coconut aminos to the pan. When the aminos have been completely absorbed, add the remainder of your ingredients.

Cook for 15 to 20 minutes on medium low heat, checking to see if the pumpkin pieces are soft. When the pumpkin has reached the proper tenderness, carefully pour everything into a high speed blender. Use a large deep spoon to assisted you with this process. Blend until smooth. Place mixture into a serving bowl.

Serve the cream of pumpkin and mushroom mix with your favorite salad, sprouts, gluten free bread or gluten free seed-like grain. Drizzle some infused oil on the top of the creamy mixture for extra flavor!

Serves around 3 to 4 bowls.

WAKAME SALAD AND FRESH PERSIMMONS

Ingredients

1 cup of dehydrated wakame

2 cups of water

1/2 cup of small diced persimmons

1/2 cup of small diced cucumbers

1/4 cup of pecans

Dressing

4 tbsp of cold press organic olive oil

1 tbsp of miso

1/2 tsp of ginger juice

1 tsp of Bragg apple cider vinegar

Himalayan salt and freshly ground pepper to taste

Instructions:

To begin the recipe, gather all the ingredients and organize your work area. Measure and pre-prep your recipe ingredients.

Add the water and the wakame to a medium size bowl and allow the wakame to rehydrate for 15-20 minutes or until ready. Once rehydrated, drain the water from the wakame. Add the wakame to a mixing bowl, along with the small diced persimmons and cucumbers.

To prepare the dressing, add all the dressing ingredients into a small mixing bowl and whisk the ingredients until they are fully combined.

Pour 2 to 3 tablespoons of the dressing into the bowl of wakame, persimmons, and cucumbers. Toss all the salad ingredients to thoroughly incorporate the dressing mixture. Add fresh or roasted pecans for extra protein.

Plate salad into individual bowls and serve with your favorite plant-based main or side dish.

Serves around 1 or 2 bowls.

KALE SALAD

Ingredients:

4 cups of chopped kale

1 cup of watermelon radish

pink peppercorn flakes for garnish

Dressing

1 tbsp of raw tahini

1 tbsp of sesame oil

6 tbsp of cold press organic olive oil

1/4 tsp of ginger juice

1 tbsp of Bragg apple cider vinegar

1 drop of liquid stevia

Himalayan salt and freshly ground black pepper to taste

Instructions:

To begin the recipe, gather all the ingredients and organize your work area. Measure and pre-prep your recipe ingredients.

Next, combine all the ingredients for the dressing in a small mixing bowl and whisk until smooth.

Add the kale and watermelon radish to the mixing bowl. Pour 2 to 3 tablespoons of the dressing, or as much as you desire, into the salad. Mix well.

Plate and garnish the dish with pink peppercorn flakes. Serve the salad with your favorite side dish, grain or plant based protein.

Serves around 2 people.

ROASTED CHLORELLA CAULIFLOWER

Ingredients:

1 cauliflower head or 5 cups of chopped cauliflower

6 mashed garlic cloves

1 tbsp of Chlorella

2 tbsp of coconut oil

1/2 lemon

Sea salt and freshly ground pepper to taste

Instructions:

To begin the recipe, gather all the ingredients and organize your work area. Measure and pre-prep your recipe ingredients.

Add all the ingredients into a large mixing bowl and combine well.

Preheat your oven to 370 degrees Fahrenheit.

Spread your Chlorella Cauliflower evenly onto a baking tray. Roast the cauliflower on one side for approximately 10 minutes or until they are lightly browned. Carefully turn the cauliflower over with a spatula and continue roasting for another 5 to 10 minutes.

Plate your Chlorella Cauliflower. Serve with your favorite side dish, grain, plant based protein or dressing. Serves around 2 to 3 people.

CHOCOLATE COVERED BUÑUELO COOKIES

Ingredients:

2 cups of medium diced Japanese sweet potatoes

1 cup of dried shredded coconut

1 cup of ground buckwheat groats

1/2 tsp of vanilla powder or 1 tsp of vanilla extract

4 tbsp of ground chia seeds

pinch of sea salt

1/3 cup of ground buckwheat for dusting the area of work

Chocolate Cream

1 cup of melted coconut oil

4 tbsp of cacao powder or as much as you desired

pinch of vanilla powder or 1/2 tsp of vanilla extract

maple syrup to taste

pinch of sea salt

1/2 tsp of lemon juice

Note- if you are using alcohol vanilla extract, omit lemon juice.

coconut flakes to garnish

Instructions:

To begin the recipe, gather all the ingredients and organize your work area. Measure and pre-prep your recipe ingredients.

In a medium size pot, bring 2 to 3 cups of water to a boil. Arrange the sweet potatoes in a bamboo steamer basket and carefully place the basket on top of the pot.

Note- Make sure to add more water, if needed, to avoid burning the pot.

Allow the sweet potatoes to steam until soft. When the sweet potatoes are fork tender, remove them from the pot and allow them to cool.

Once the sweet potatoes have cooled off, place them in a mixing bowl and mash them with a fork. They should be very soft and easily mashed. Add the coconut oil, pinch of salt, vanilla, ground buckwheat and ground chia seeds to the mashed sweet potatoes. Mix well and start working mixture into a dough like consistency.

If the texture of the dough is not firm and flexible, add more ground chia seeds and ground buckwheat.

Note- Japanese sweet potatoes are very sweet, naturally. I do not add any extra sugar to the dough. If you desire extra sweetness, you may add some stevia, honey or maple syrup to taste.

Leave the dough in the mixing bowl, cover and allow it to rest inside the refrigerator for 15 minutes.

When you reach the 15-minute mark, remove the dough from the refrigerator and get ready to work.

Divide the dough into two pieces and cover the other half.

Grab a small piece of the dough in your hands and shape dough into a little bowl. Dust a pizza roller and your area of work with ground buckwheat and roll the little bowl to form a small disk shape. If you want to be fancier, use a cookie cutter to achieve a perfectly round shape

Note- Have fun and be creative!! You can create any shapes you like. Involve your children in the process, too.

Preheat your oven to 375 degrees Fahrenheit. Add 1 tsp of coconut oil to a baking tray and distribute evenly over the entire tray.

*Note- Please use parchment paper to bake the buñuelo cookies if it feels more comfortable to you.

Place all your buñuelo cookies on the baking tray and bake on one side for 5 to 7 minutes or until they are lightly browned. Turn buñuelo cookies over and continue cooking for another 5 to 7 minutes.

Once the buñuelo cookies are baked, allow them to cool off. Place them in the refrigerator for 10 to 15 minutes.

Cacao Cream

To prepare the cacao cream gently add all the cacao cream ingredients into a high speed blender and blend until completely smooth.

Now, the really fun part is about to start! Place the cacao cream in a small container and the coconut flakes in another one. Dip a buñuelo cookie into the cacao cream, making sure it is completely coated.

Immediately, sprinkle the coconut flakes over a portion of your favorite area.

Place the buñuelo cookies covered in cacao cream and coconut flakes on your favorite tray and what can I say, ENJOY!!!!

Serves around 15 to 20 depending on the size.

OMEGA 3 NO ICE CREAM-ICE CREAM

Ingredients:

1/2 cup of frozen cranberries

1 cup of frozen strawberries

2 tbsp of Udos 3-6-9 DHA oil

2 date

1 tsp to 1 tbsp of Sacha Inchi Powder (optional)

pinch of Himalayan salt

a splash of the nut milk of your choice if any liquid is needed.

Instructions:

  To begin the recipe, gather all the ingredients and organize your work area. Measure and pre-prep your recipe ingredients.

  Add all your ingredients into a high speed blender and blend until you reach an ice cream consistency.

  Serve with your favorite raw cookies! Serves 1 to 2 people.

CACAO SWEET POTATO BROWNIES

Ingredients:

2 1/2 cups of pecans

1 tbsp of baking soda

1 tbsp of Bragg apple cider vinegar

1/2 cup of coconut milk

Note - If your area is high in humidity, ensure to use only half of the coconut milk to achieve a brownie batter consistency. However, these brownies are still delicious if a little extra moisture is present after baking!

Maple syrup to taste

1 tbsp of vanilla extract

3/4 cup of cacao powder

1 cup of Yams (sweet potatoes)

pinch of salt

coconut flakes for garnish

Instructions:

To begin the recipe, gather all the ingredients and organize your work area. Measure and pre-prep your recipe ingredients.

On medium high heat, pour 2 to 3 cups of water into a medium size pot. Bring water to a boil. Arrange the diced sweet potatoes in a bamboo steamer and place the steamer on top of the pot. Allow the sweet potatoes to steam for 5 to 10 minutes. When you pierce the sweet potatoes with a fork, they should fall off, but still, retain a firm shape.

Note- The smaller the dice of the sweet potatoes, the faster they cook. Be careful not to overcook.

Next, place the pecans in a food processor and grind them finely to a flour consistency.

Note- Do not over process or the pecans will turn into butter.

Place the pecan flour in a mixing bowl and add the remainder of your dry ingredients.

In a separate mixing bowl, mash the sweet potatoes with a fork and add all the wet ingredients to the mashed sweet potatoes. Mix until ingredients are thoroughly blended. Next, combine the dry and wet ingredients, until a brownie batter consistency is achieved.

Preheat the oven to 350 degrees Fahrenheit.

*Note- Please use parchment paper to bake the sweet potato brownies if it feels more comfortable to you.

Sprinkle coconut flakes into a brownie baking tray. Gently spread on the brownie batter. When the batter is evenly distributed over the entire baking tray, place in the oven and allow the batter to cook for approximately 15 to 20 minutes.

Note- Depending on the humidity content of your area and the type of oven, you may need a few minutes more or less of cooking time. Keep a careful eye on your brownies while baking!

Insert a toothpick into the brownie batter to test if they are done. The brownies are ready to pull out of the oven when the toothpick comes out clean and dry. Allow the brownies to cool off. As they do so, you will notice the brownies will cool to a more crunchy consistency.

Serve with your favorite vegan ice cream or eat by itself as a healthy treat!

Serves around 12 mini brownies.

THANK YOU

This book is dedicated to my Father Noel Gorgoy, my Mother Belkys Reyes, my Brother Noel Jose Gorgoy, my Sister Yunary Gorgoy for being my everything!

To Chris Tollette for the love, the support and for being my rock in every moment, no matter how easy or hard it might be. For materializing this vision with me since day one, taking the most beautiful pictures and helping me through out this crazy idea of creating a book.

To Shelly Tollette and Jim Tollette, for the love and the support. For editing this book, making sense of every word and making it sound so beautiful.

To all my friends and family.

To my amazing Bella and Papi for teaching me unconditional love and always inspiring me. I love you.

To the team of educators of the Professional Plant Based Certification Course of Rouxbe Online Cooking School lead by world-renowned plant-based chef educator Chad Sarno. For the amazing and transformative course you guys put together.

   To you, for your love and support. For helping me spread the message and being part of this new adventure in my life.

   Peace, blessing, and love to you and let's change the world one bite at a time.